DRAW WITH WILL

WILL SLINEY

FOR IAN AND LUCY. THANK YOU FOR HELPING TO BRING THE JOY OF ART TO SO MANY KIDS AROUND THE WORLD.

First published in Great Britain in 2025 by Gallery Kids, an imprint of Simon & Schuster UK Ltd

Text and illustrations © 2025 Will Sliney
Colour by Rachelle Rosenberg
Designed by Kathryn Slack

1 3 5 7 9 10 8 6 4 2

Simon & Schuster UK Ltd
1st Floor, 222 Gray's Inn Road
London WC1X 8HB

Simon & Schuster: Celebrating 100 Years of Publishing in 2024

www.simonandschuster.co.uk
www.simonandschuster.com.au
www.simonandschuster.co.in

Simon & Schuster Australia, Sydney
Simon & Schuster India, New Delhi

A CIP catalogue record for this book
is available from the British Library.

PB ISBN 978-1-3985-3496-4
eBook ISBN 978-1-3985-3497-1

Printed and bound in China by RR Donnelley
Asia Printing Solutions Limited Company,
Dongguan, Guangdong

MIX
Paper | Supporting
responsible forestry
FSC
www.fsc.org   FSC® C144853

HOW TO USE THIS BOOK

ON THESE LEFT-HAND PAGES YOU'LL FIND SOME STEP-BY-STEP TUTORIALS. THESE WILL TEACH YOU HOW TO DRAW THINGS NEEDED FOR EACH PAGE . . .

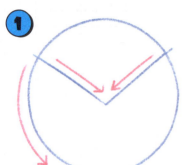

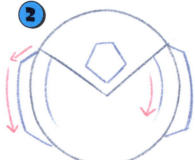

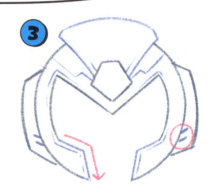

WE WILL ALWAYS START EACH TUTORIAL BY SHOWING YOU THE SIMPLE LEVEL 1 SHAPES. LIKE THIS CIRCLE, AND A POINTED LINE THAT WILL BE THE BROW OF THE HELMET.

WE WILL BUILD ON TOP OF THE DRAWING WITH SMALLER LEVEL 2 DETAILS. USUALLY, THE SHAPES GET MORE COMPLEX, BUT I WILL GUIDE YOU THROUGH IT ALL.

THE LAST STEP IS ABOUT THE SMALL LEVEL 3 DETAILS. THESE ADD THE FINAL, IMPORTANT TOUCHES THAT TAKE A DRAWING FROM GOOD TO GREAT.

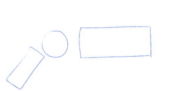

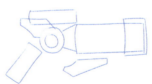

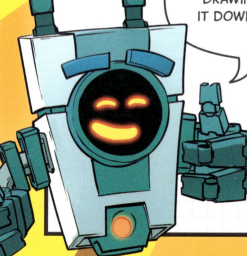

NO MATTER HOW HARD THE DRAWING IS, LIKE THIS TRICKY BLASTER DRAWING, WE WILL ALWAYS BREAK IT DOWN INTO SIMPLE SHAPES AND DIFFERENT LEVELS.

AND I'LL BE HERE EVERY STEP OF THE WAY TO HELP.

I MEAN . . . IT'S NOT LIKE SOMETHING CRAZY IS GOING TO HAPPEN TO ME TO GET IN THE WAY NOW IS IT?

HOW TO DRAW
ALIEN EYES AND MONSTER TEETH

LET'S HAVE SOME FUN AND DRAW SOME CREEPY EYES AND TEETH. FIRST, I WILL SHOW YOU HOW TO MAKE AN EYE LOOK SINISTER.

ALIEN EYES

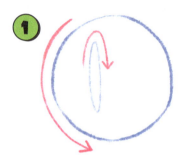

1 LET'S DRAW A CIRCLE FOR THE EYE, AND A THIN OVAL FOR A PUPIL.

2 USING A SEMICIRCLE, DRAW A LOWER EYELID THROUGH THE EYE. ERASE ANYTHING BELOW OUR NEW LINE AND COLOUR IN THE PUPIL.

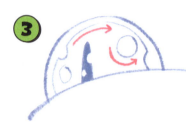

3 MAKE THE EYE SHINY BY DRAWING CIRCULAR HIGHLIGHTS AND A CIRCULAR RIM LIGHT LINE. YOU CAN EVEN MAKE HIGHLIGHTS IN THE PUPIL USING AN ERASER.

MONSTER TEETH

THIS IS A CREATURE FROM OUR IMAGINATION. DRAW EYES IN ANY SHAPE YOU WANT, AS LONG AS YOU CAN IMAGINE IT. NOW CHECK OUT THESE TEETH.

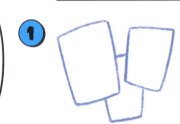

1 LET'S DRAW A FEW TOGETHER HERE, BUT HAVE THEM DIFFERENT SIZES.

PRO TIP
IF YOU WANT TO MAKE YOUR MONSTER LOOK FIERCE, THEN SHARPEN IT'S TEETH WITH POINTY EDGES.

2 DRAW THIN LINES ON THE TOOTH FOR TEXTURE. PUT IN A LITTLE SEMICIRCLE TO SHOW WHERE THE TOOTH MEETS THE GUM.

3 THEN ADD SALIVA BY DRAWING THESE LITTLE CIRCLES FALLING FROM THE TOOTH.

HOW TO DRAW A THINGAMABOB DEVICE

LOOKS LIKE WILL IS IN TROUBLE AND HE NEEDS AN ESCAPOMATIC THINGAMABOB. LET'S DRAW HIM ONE.

1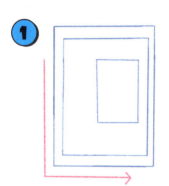

LET'S START WITH SIMPLE RECTANGLES TO BLOCK OUT THE LEVEL 1 SHAPES.

2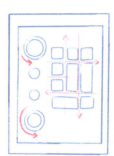

NOW DIVIDE ONE RECTANGLE INTO SMALLER SHAPED BUTTONS. ADD IN SOME CIRCULAR BUTTONS.

3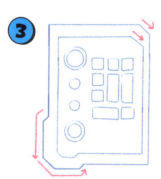

THEN, TO MAKE IT FUTURISTIC, I'LL MAKE THESE CORNERS ANGULAR.

TO TAKE OUR DRAWING UP A NOTCH, LET'S DRAW THAT IN THREE DIMENSIONS, OR 3D, WHERE WE BRING VOLUME TO OUR SHAPES.

4

2D

START BY DRAWING A SIMPLE SQUARE AND A CIRCLE.

5 **3D**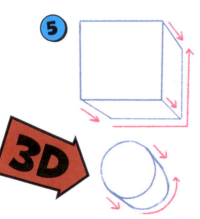

TO TURN A SQUARE INTO A CUBE, OR A CIRCLE INTO A CYLINDER, WE ADD VOLUME LIKE THIS.

6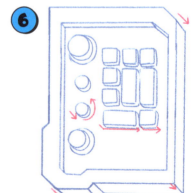

NOW LET'S APPLY THAT TO OUR DEVICE.

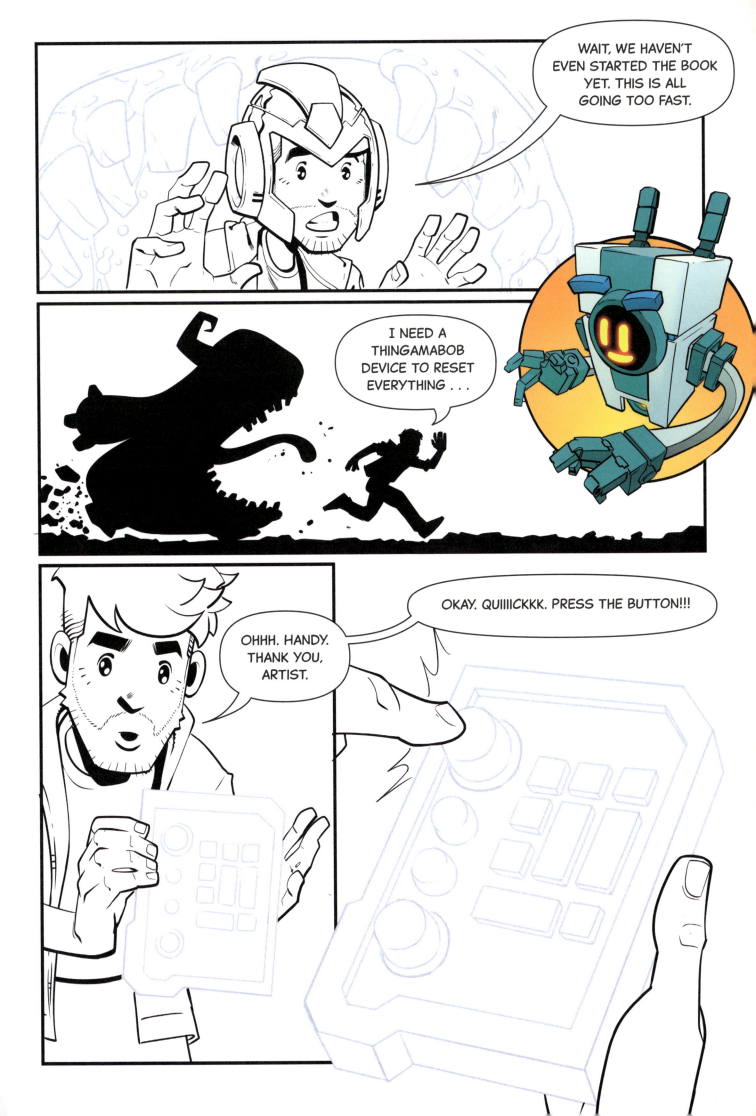

CREATE AND DRAW YOUR OWN CRAZY THINGAMABOB DEVICE HERE

CHAPTER 1
SIMPLE SHAPES

MAKING DRAWDROID WITH SIMPLE SHAPES

OKAY, PHEW, THANKS FOR HELPING ME ESCAPE. BUT I THINK YOU ACTUALLY DREW ME A TIME-TRAVEL DEVICEAMABOB INSTEAD OF AN ESCAPOMATIC CONTROLLER.

WHICH MEANS WE HAVE GONE BACK IN TIME TO BEFORE I MADE DRAWDROID.

THAT'S OKAY THOUGH. WE CAN BUILD IT TOGETHER. LET'S TAKE THINGS A LITTLE SLOWER AND START PRACTISING SOME SIMPLE SHAPES.

LEVEL 1

1

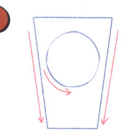

LET'S START WITH A TAPERED RECTANGLE AND A CIRCLE.

'TAPERING' IS MAKING ONE SIDE SMALLER THAN THE OTHER. OUR BOTTOM IS SMALLER THAN OUR TOP.

2

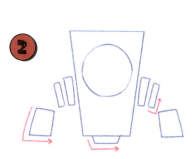

NOW I'LL ADD IN A FEW MORE SIMPLE SHAPES TO MAKE MORE OF DRAWDROID'S DETAILS.

LEVEL 2

1

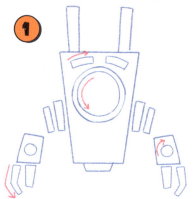

LEVEL 2 SHAPES ARE OFTEN SIMPLE SHAPES BUT SMALLER. LIKE THESE EYEBROWS AND FINGERS.

2

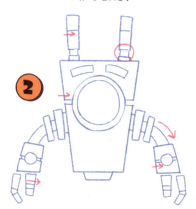

START BREAKING UP THE LARGE SHAPES AND ADD IN THE CURVES FOR THE ARM.

LEVEL 3

1

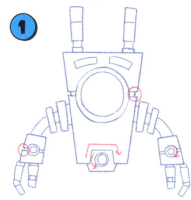

LEVEL 3 DETAILS TAKE YOUR DRAWING FROM GOOD TO GREAT! DRAW IN THE SMALL DETAILS LIKE THE SMALL CIRCLES.

2

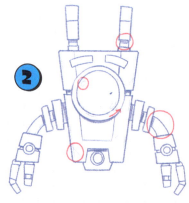

TINY LINES ADD TEXTURE AND COSMETIC DETAILS. FINALLY, ADD SOME SHADOWS, SOME HIGHLIGHTS.

DRAWING IN THREE DIMENSIONS

LET'S TAKE DRAWDROID FROM 2D TO 3D BY GIVING HIM VOLUME AND SHAPE.

START WITH THIS SIMPLE SHAPE, WHICH IS OUR TAPERED RECTANGLE, BUT IT'S DRAWN AT AN ANGLE.

THEN WE CAN MAKE THE SHAPE 3D BY ADDING IN VOLUME.

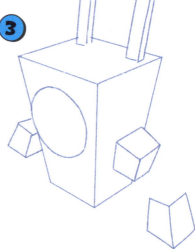

I'LL BLOCK OUT THE DESIGN FURTHER BY ADDING IN THESE LEVEL 1 3D SHAPES.

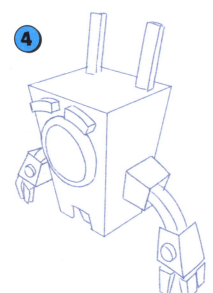

EACH ELEMENT WE DREW IN 2D, WE CAN RECREATE IN 3D HERE.

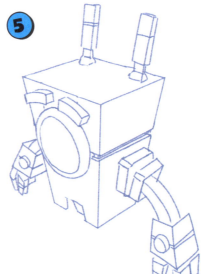

THEN, WHEN IT'S BLOCKED OUT, WE CAN ADD THE LEVEL 3 DETAILS ON TOP OF THE SHAPES.

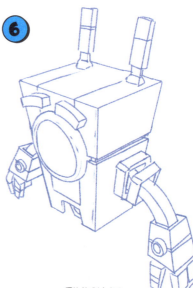

FINISH IT OFF WITH THE SAME TEXTURES AS THE 2D DRAWING.

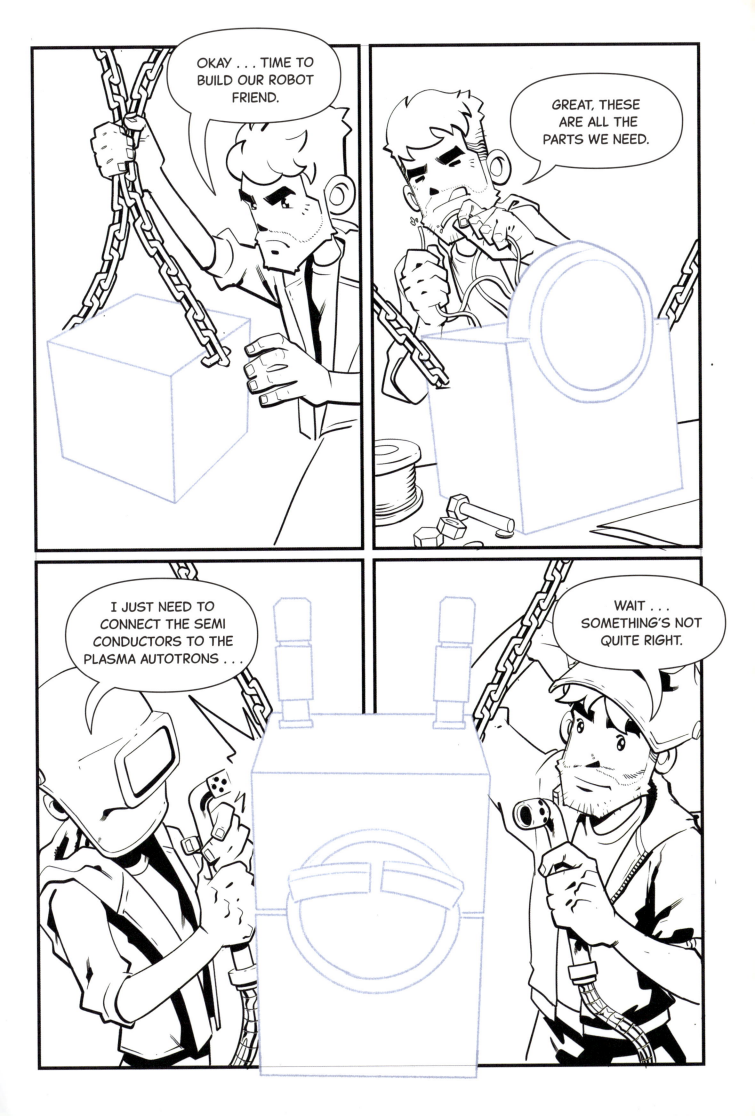

BRINGING SIMPLE SHAPES TO LIFE

HMMM, HE IS STILL NOT ALIVE . . . HE JUST LOOKS LIKE A COLLECTION OF BOXES. LET'S ADD CURVES TO BRING MOVEMENT.

1

LET'S DRAW A RECTANGLE, OUR MAIN SHAPE FOR DRAWDROID.

2

EXCEPT INSTEAD OF DRAWING IT WITH STRAIGHT LINES, LET'S ADD CURVES.

3
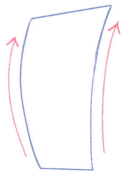

THE MORE YOU CURVE THE SIDES, THE MORE EXTREME THE MOVEMENT.

4

EACH ELEMENT WE DREW IN 2D, WE CAN RECREATE IN 3D HERE.

5
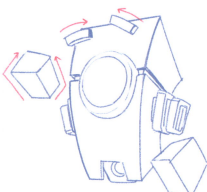

THEN, WHEN IT'S BLOCKED OUT, WE CAN ADD THE LEVEL 3 DETAILS.

6
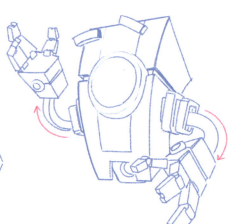

FINISH IT OFF WITH THE SAME TEXTURES AS THE 2D DRAWING.

DRAW YOUR OWN ROBOT USING ALL THE TECHNIQUES YOU HAVE LEARNED. YOU CAN EITHER DRAW THEM IN 2D OR 3D.

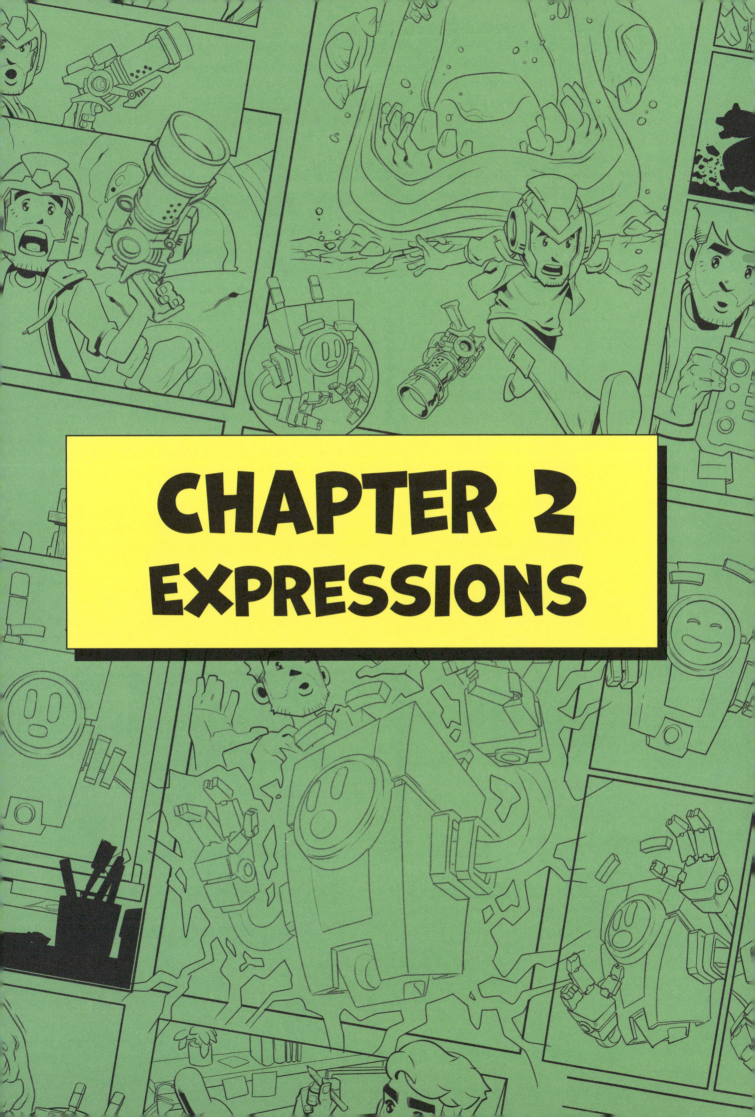

CHAPTER 2
EXPRESSIONS

HOW TO DRAW EXPRESSIONS

PLEASED TO MEET YOU . . . I AM—

DRAWDROID, YEAH WE KNOW . . . HMMMM, IT SEEMS YOU ARE MISSING SOMETHING.

LET'S GIVE DRAWDROID SOME ROBOTIC FACIAL FEATURES SO THEY CAN COMMUNICATE MORE. IN FACT, YOU CAN PICK WHICHEVER STYLE YOU WOULD LIKE. THEY JUST NEED EYES AND A MOUTH. HERE ARE SOME EXAMPLES OF DIFFERENT WAYS YOU COULD DRAW.

THIS IS PIXEL ART. EACH PART OF THE FACE IS DRAWN BY COMBINING INDIVIDUAL SQUARES TOGETHER.

THESE ARE EMOJIS. THEY SHOW HOW EMOTIONS ARE ALWAYS BEST EXPRESSED: WITH A FACE.

HERE IS AN EXAMPLE OF SOME ANIME-STYLE EXPRESSIONS. ANIME IS KNOW AS ONE OF THE MOST EXPRESSIVE TYPES OF ART.

DRAW YOUR OWN EXPRESSION

WHENEVER DRAWDROID IS MISSING A FACE IN THE BOOK, DRAW IN YOUR OWN EXPRESSION.

HOW TO DRAW HUMAN EXPRESSIONS

WHOA WHOA WHOA . . . IT'S NOT JUST MY EMOTIONS YOU CAN CONTROL. WE CAN DO THE SAME FOR WILL.

BUT I ALREADY HAVE A FACE . . . MMMMPH!

1

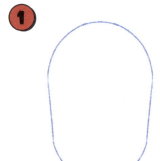

LET'S START WITH OUR LEVEL 1 SHAPE. DRAW AN OVAL FOR THE HEAD.

2

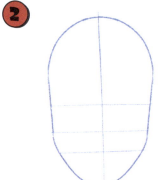

DIVIDE IT WITH GRID LINES TO HELP US FIGURE OUT WHERE TO PLACE THE FACIAL FEATURES.

3

DRAW THE EYES, NOSE AND MOUTH IN ANY STYLE YOU LIKE. I'M KEEPING IT NICE AND SIMPLE.

4

ONCE THE FEATURES ARE IN PLACE, IT'S TIME TO ADD IN THE HAIR AND, IN THIS CASE, THE BEARD.

5

EXPRESSIONS CAN BE FUN. HERE IS A BAMBOOZLED WILL WITH A SHOCKED MOUTH AND SPIRAL EYES.

6

OR HOW ABOUT AN ANGRY WILL WITH HIS EYES SHUT AND GRITTED TEETH?

HOW TO DRAW ALIEN EXPRESSIONS

OH GREAT . . . IT'S OUR ALIEN MONSTER!

HERE IS WHERE WE CAN GET REEEEALLY EXPRESSIVE. NOW THAT WE KNOW HOW TO DRAW THE DIFFERENT EXPRESSIONS, LET'S HAVE FUN AND REALLY PUSH THE POSE.

START BY DRAWING OUR SIMPLE EYE, COMPLETE WITH THE THIN OVAL AND THE ROUND HIGHLIGHTS.

CHANGE ITS SHAPE WITH THE EYELIDS TO MAKE IT POINTY.

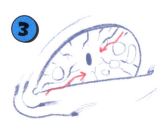

THESE LITTLE LINES ARE BLOOD VESSELS. THEY HELP WITH THE SCARY LOOK.

WE COULD DRAW IN A NICE BIG SMILE BUT . . .

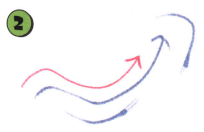

WHY DON'T WE MAKE IT CROOKED BY HAVING ONE SIDE GO UP?

THEIR TEETH ARE TOO BIG AT TIMES TO FIT UNDER THE LIPS, SO WE CAN HAVE THEM POKING OUT.

PRO TIP
POINTY = ANGRY
ROUND = FRIENDLY

WE CAN CONVEY AN UNDERLYING EMOTION HERE, WHERE THE SMILE AND EYES ARE A LITTLE DEVIOUS. INSTEAD OF HAVING THEM OPEN LIKE WILL'S WERE FOR HIS HAPPY EXPRESSION, LET'S DRAW THEM THIN, ALMOST AS IF THEY ARE HIDING SOMETHING.

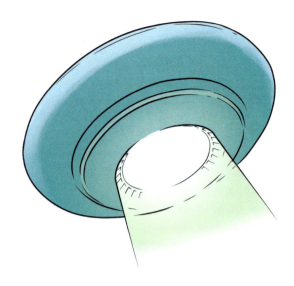

PRACTISE DRAWING YOUR OWN EXPRESSIONS HERE. IT CAN BE AN ALIEN, HUMAN OR ROBOT . . . YOU CHOOSE!

CHAPTER 3
CREATURES

HOW TO DRAW
AN OCTOPUS

OUR STORY NEEDS SOME CRAZY CREATURE CREATIONS TO COME OUT OF THE ALIEN SHIP.

LET'S MAKE SOME BY FINDING ANIMALS IN NATURE AND MAKING THEM LOOK CRAZY BY COMBINING ELEMENTS.

FIRST, WE ARE GOING TO DRAW THIS OCTOPUS. LIKE ALWAYS, WE WILL START BY DRAWING SIMPLE SHAPES.

LET'S START WITH AN OVAL, BUT WE ARE GOING TO TAPER IT SO IT IS THINNER AT THE BOTTOM.

THE EYES SIT ON THE HEAD LIKE THIS. DRAW IN A LARGE SEMICIRCLE FOR A HUGE MOUTH.

THEN ADD IN SOME FINER DETAILS WITH THE EYE-LASHES, PUPILS, TEETH AND TEXTURE.

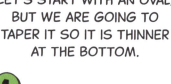

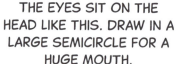

NOW: THE REALLY FUN PART. WE CAN DRAW THE TENTACLES AND HAVE THEM SPIN AROUND IN ANY SHAPE WE WANT.

MAKE SURE THESE SHAPES FLOW USING WAVY LINES.

WHEN WE SEE ANY PART OF THE UNDERSIDE OF THE TENTACLE, WE CAN ADD IN THESE SUCKERS BY DRAWING THESE LITTLE CIRCLES.

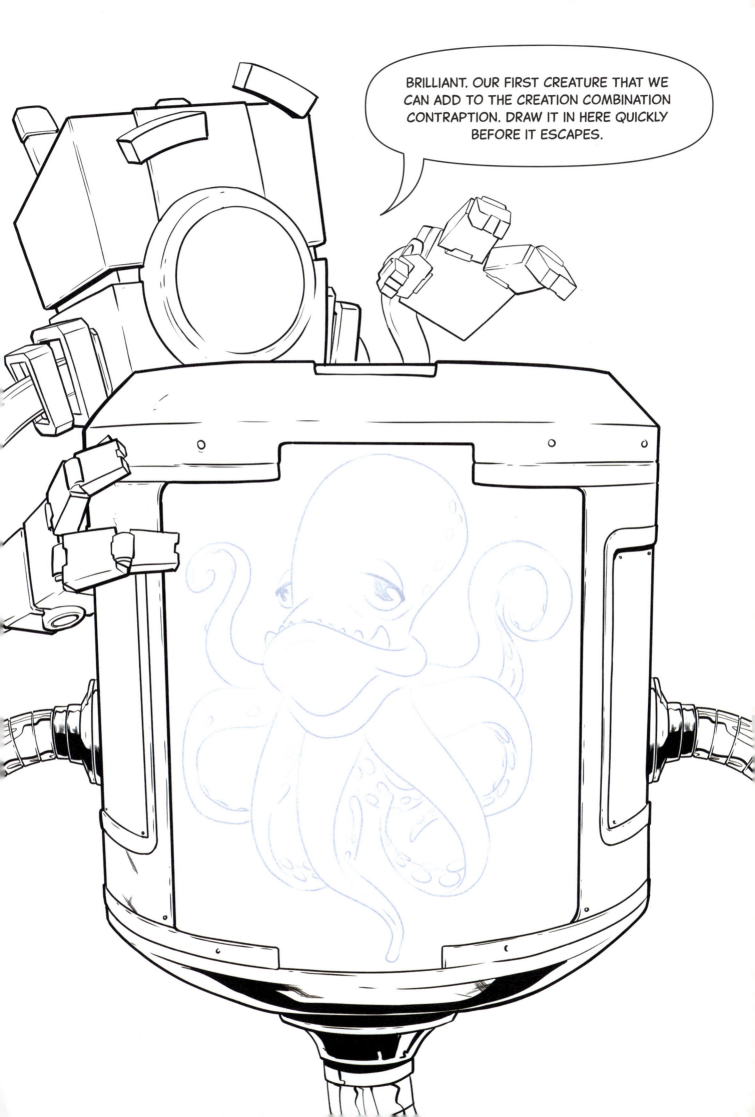

HOW TO DRAW
A WASP AND A CAT

IN ORDER TO COMBINE CREATURES, WE ARE GOING TO NEED MORE THAN ONE. LET'S DRAW A FEW MORE.

WASP

1

START DRAWING THE WASP BY DRAWING A FEW POINTY, CURVED LEVEL 1 CIRCLES.

2

ADD IN FUR WITH TRIANGULAR CLUMPS AND POINTY, LEGS.

3

THE WINGS OF A WASP CAN BE DRAWN WITH BROKEN AND JAGGED LINES.

CAT

1

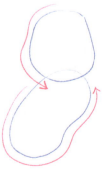

DRAW IN THESE SIMPLE SHAPES. FOR THE BODY, TILT THE OVAL AT AN ANGLE.

2

THE CAT HAS A HEART-SHAPED NOSE AND A CURVY TAIL. WE USE LOTS OF *SEMICIRCLES* TO MAKE THE SHAPES FOR LEVEL 2.

3

THEN FOR LEVEL 3, INSTEAD OF SOFT SEMICIRCLES, DRAW THE HAIR TEXTURE WITH POINTY, JAGGED LINES.

HOW TO COMBINE PARTS TO CREATE CREATURES

NOW IT'S TIME FOR THE FUN PART. WE ARE GOING TO COMBINE AND SWAP THEIR PARTS. BY TAKING THE PARTS OF NORMAL, EVERYDAY CREATURES AND SWAPPING THEM AROUND, WE CAN MAKE SOME GREAT NEW DESIGNS.

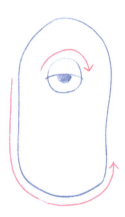

DRAW A SIMPLE, LONG OVAL FOR THE BODY SHAPE OF OUR NEW ALIEN CREATURE. LET'S GIVE HIM ONE LARGE EYE THAT'S HALF OPEN.

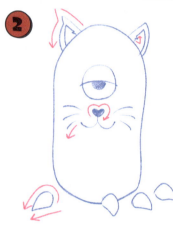

NEXT, I'M GOING TO USE THE CAT'S NOSE, WHISKERS AND EARS, AS WELL AS THE WASP'S POINTY FEET.

FINALLY, ADD THE FURRY TEXTURE WE DREW ON THE WASP ALL OVER OUR CREATURE'S BODY.

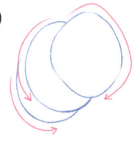

LET'S CREATE A SECOND FIGURE BY COMBINING THREE SIMPLE CIRCLE SHAPES.

THEN, DRAW IN THE OCTOPUS'S MOUTH, AND THE WASPS EYES AND ANTENNAE.

LASTLY, LETS MAKE IT FLY WITH THE WASP'S WINGS AND HAVE THE OCTOPUS'S LEGS DANGLE DOWN.

CHAPTER 4
SUPERHEROES

HOW TO DRAW SUPERHERO ARMOUR

THERE IS ABSOLUTELY NO CHANCE I AM GOING TO ESCAPE THESE ALIENS WITHOUT HELP FROM YOU.

SO I THINK IT'S TIME TO POWER ME UP WITH SOME AWESOME SUPERHERO ARMOUR.

LET'S DRAW THIS CHEST PIECE AND SHOULDER PADS. THE GOAL HERE IS TO EXAGGERATE THE FORM AND MAKE OUR HERO LOOK BIGGER AND STRONGER.

NOT AN EASY THING TO DO!

LET'S ADD SOME TECHNICAL PARTS AS LEVEL 2 SHAPES, LIKE THESE BELTS AND STRAPS.

THEN WE CAN ADD MORE DETAIL WITH THE SMALLER LEVEL 3 DETAILS TO TAKE OUR ARMOUR FROM GOOD TO GREAT.

HOW TO DESIGN
COSTUMES

LOOKS LIKE YOU ARE MISSING SOMETHING FROM YOUR COSTUME THERE, WILL.

IT'S TOP HEAVY AND LOOKS LIKE A TRIANGLE WHEN YOU SEE THE SILHOUETTE.

LET'S BULK OUT THE BODY AND DRAW ON SOME GLOVES AND BOOTS.

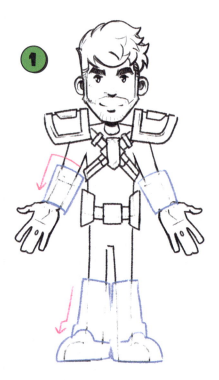

LET'S DRAW IN SOME BULKY BOOTS AND GAUNTLETS TO BALANCE THE SILHOUETTE.

WHAT'S A SUPERHERO WITHOUT A MASK AND SOME BULKY KNEE-PADS?

THE LEVEL 3 DETAILS, WHICH ARE THE DESIGNS THAT WE PLACE ON THE BOOTS, GAUNTLETTS AND CHEST, FINISH THINGS OFF.

CHAPTER 5
SUPERPOWERS

HOW TO DRAW SUPERPOWERS

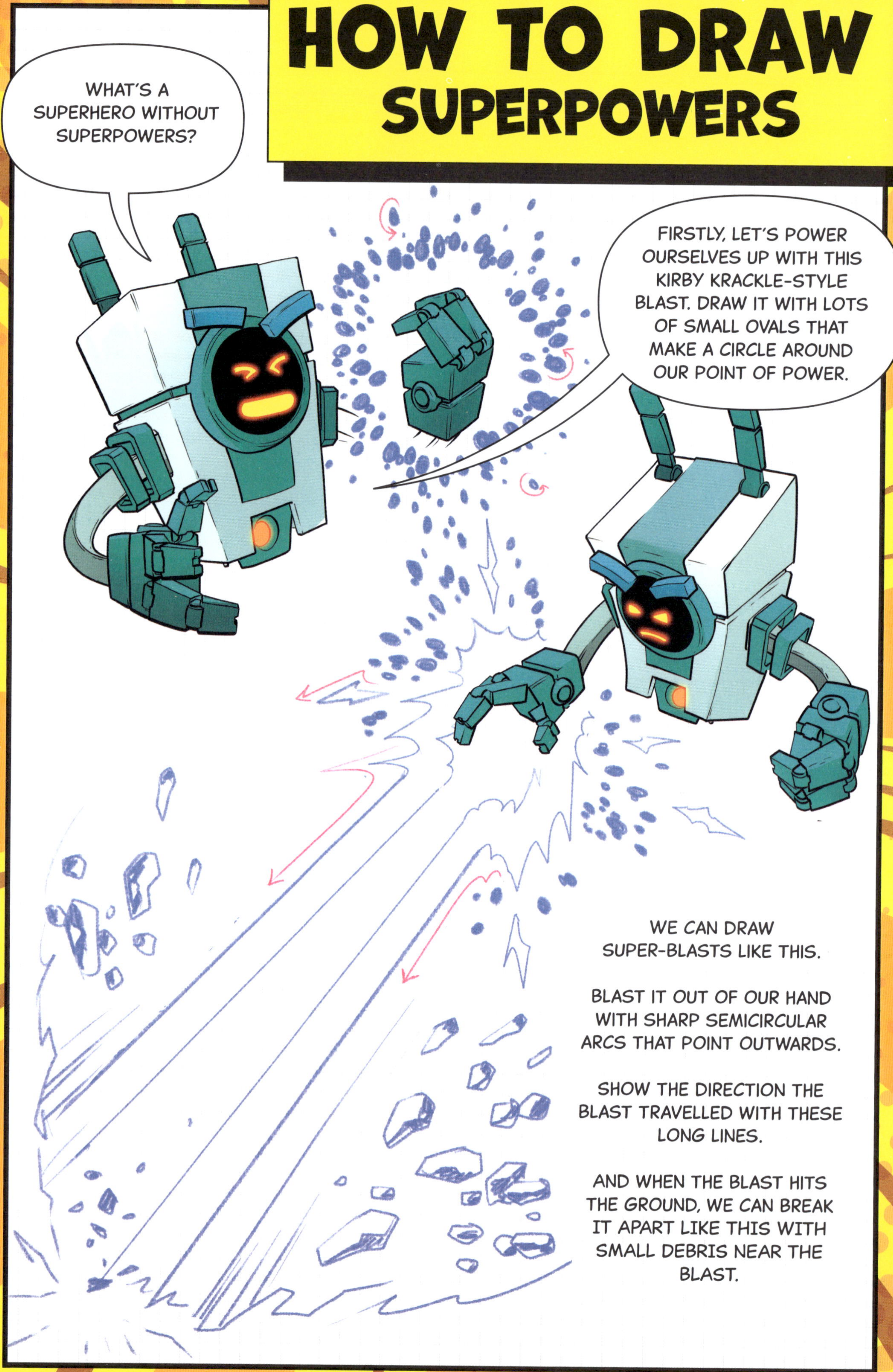

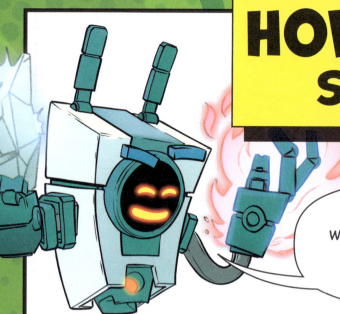

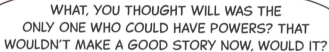

WHAT, YOU THOUGHT WILL WAS THE ONLY ONE WHO COULD HAVE POWERS? THAT WOULDN'T MAKE A GOOD STORY NOW, WOULD IT?

LET'S GIVE OUR ALIEN ICE POWERS SO IT CAN EMIT A FREEZE BLAST.

TO DRAW A LARGE CHUNK OF ICE, START WITH A SIMPLE OVAL.

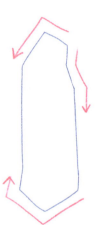

NOW, CHANGE THE EDGES OF OUR SHAPE TO SHARP, STRAIGHT LINES.

ICE HAS LOTS OF EDGES AND HIGHLIGHTS, SO ADD MORE ANGLED SHAPES AND BURSTS OF LIGHT.

FOR FLAMES, WE NEED TO COMBINE SEMICIRCLES. PUT TWO TOGETHER TO MAKE A SHARP POINT.

DRAW MORE OF THESE SHAPES RISING UP. KEEP USING SEMICIRCLES THAT COMBINE TO A POINT.

SOME PARTS OF THE MAIN FLAME BREAK AWAY AND FLOAT INTO THE AIR. AT THE BASE OF THE FLAME DRAW IN SOME SMALL, DARK SHAPES.

HOW TO DRAW SUPERSPEED

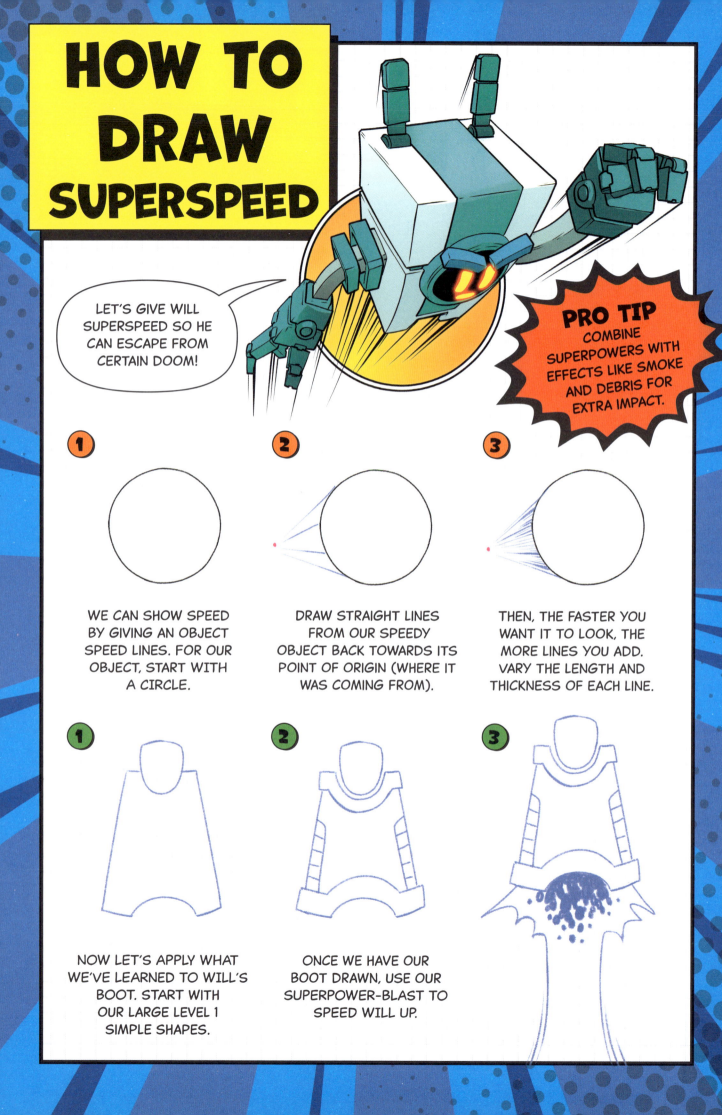

LET'S GIVE WILL SUPERSPEED SO HE CAN ESCAPE FROM CERTAIN DOOM!

PRO TIP COMBINE SUPERPOWERS WITH EFFECTS LIKE SMOKE AND DEBRIS FOR EXTRA IMPACT.

1 WE CAN SHOW SPEED BY GIVING AN OBJECT SPEED LINES. FOR OUR OBJECT, START WITH A CIRCLE.

2 DRAW STRAIGHT LINES FROM OUR SPEEDY OBJECT BACK TOWARDS ITS POINT OF ORIGIN (WHERE IT WAS COMING FROM).

3 THEN, THE FASTER YOU WANT IT TO LOOK, THE MORE LINES YOU ADD. VARY THE LENGTH AND THICKNESS OF EACH LINE.

1 NOW LET'S APPLY WHAT WE'VE LEARNED TO WILL'S BOOT. START WITH OUR LARGE LEVEL 1 SIMPLE SHAPES.

2 ONCE WE HAVE OUR BOOT DRAWN, USE OUR SUPERPOWER-BLAST TO SPEED WILL UP.

CHAPTER 6
SPACE

HOW TO DRAW OUTER SPACE

THIS ADVENTURE IS HEADING OUT OF THIS WORLD.

LET'S LEARN HOW TO TURN A SIMPLE SHAPE INTO A PLANET FROM OUTER SPACE.

 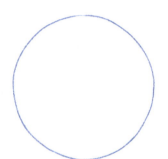

  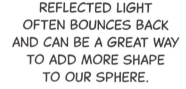

OF COURSE, WE START WITH A SIMPLE CIRCLE.

TO TURN OUR CIRCLE INTO A 3D SPHERE WE USE LIGHT AND SHADE. DRAW IN A SHADOW, AS IF THE LIGHT WAS COMING FROM ABOVE OUR SPHERE.

REFLECTED LIGHT OFTEN BOUNCES BACK AND CAN BE A GREAT WAY TO ADD MORE SHAPE TO OUR SPHERE.

  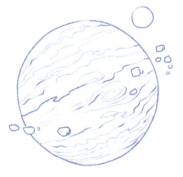

TO MAKE OUR CIRCLE LOOK LIKE THE MOON, WE NEED TO SHOW THE TEXTURE OF IT BY DRAWING LITTLE CRATERS. SOME CAN JUST BE SMALL CIRCLES.

WE CAN ALSO USE OUR ERASER TO GET RID OF SHADOWS TO SHOW THEIR HIGHLIGHTS.

LET'S DRAW A DIFFERENT PLANET BY CHANGING THE TEXTURE. USE WAVY LINES AND CIRCLES, AND GET CREATIVE!

HOW TO DRAW SOUND EFFECTS

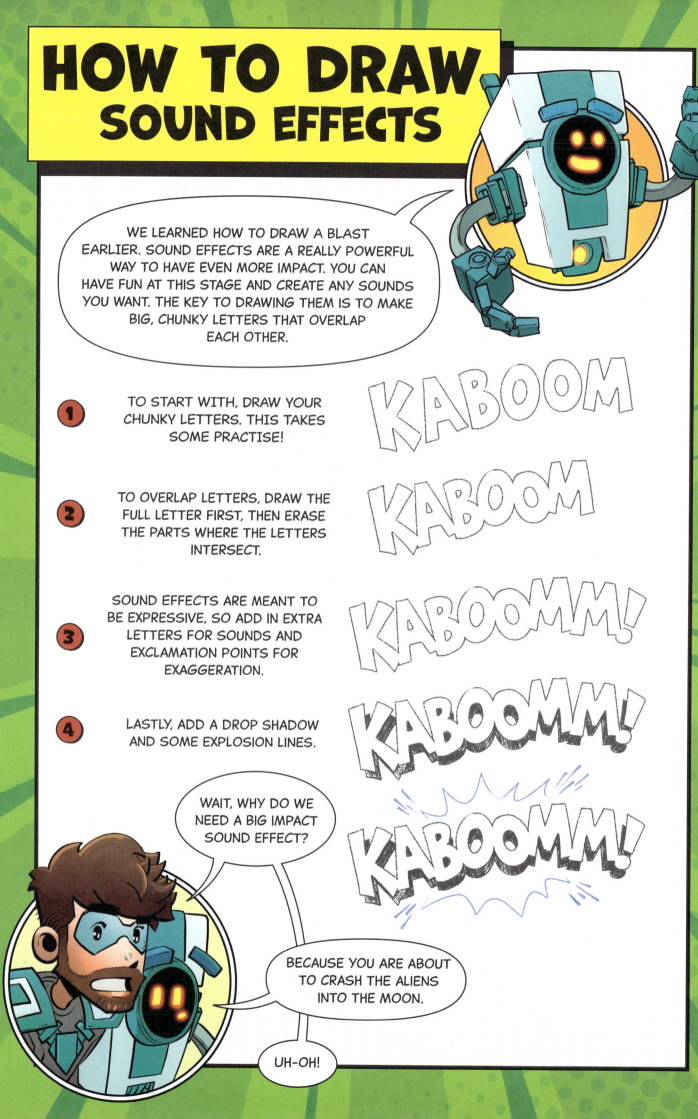

WE LEARNED HOW TO DRAW A BLAST EARLIER. SOUND EFFECTS ARE A REALLY POWERFUL WAY TO HAVE EVEN MORE IMPACT. YOU CAN HAVE FUN AT THIS STAGE AND CREATE ANY SOUNDS YOU WANT. THE KEY TO DRAWING THEM IS TO MAKE BIG, CHUNKY LETTERS THAT OVERLAP EACH OTHER.

1. TO START WITH, DRAW YOUR CHUNKY LETTERS. THIS TAKES SOME PRACTISE!

2. TO OVERLAP LETTERS, DRAW THE FULL LETTER FIRST, THEN ERASE THE PARTS WHERE THE LETTERS INTERSECT.

3. SOUND EFFECTS ARE MEANT TO BE EXPRESSIVE, SO ADD IN EXTRA LETTERS FOR SOUNDS AND EXCLAMATION POINTS FOR EXAGGERATION.

4. LASTLY, ADD A DROP SHADOW AND SOME EXPLOSION LINES.

KABOOM

KABOOM

KABOOMM!

KABOOMM!

KABOOMM!

WAIT, WHY DO WE NEED A BIG IMPACT SOUND EFFECT?

BECAUSE YOU ARE ABOUT TO CRASH THE ALIENS INTO THE MOON.

UH-OH!

HOW TO DRAW AN ASTRONAUT'S HELMET

WAIT, YOU CAN'T BREATHE IN SPACE?

OF COURSE I CAN'T BREATHE. WHY DIDN'T YOU DESIGN MY COSTUME TO HAVE A HELMET?

WELL, I DIDN'T KNOW YOU WERE GOING TO FLY INTO SPACE . . .

1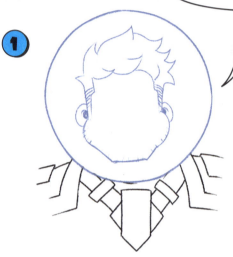

FIRST, PRACTISE DRAWING WILL'S EXPRESSION AND A CIRCLE AROUND HIS HEAD.

2

NOW, DRAW SOME SIMPLE SHAPES TO MAKE IT LOOK LIKE THE CIRCLE IS PART OF HIS SUIT.

3

GASP!!

LEVEL 2 DETAILS WILL REALLY HELP THIS. THESE SHAPES ARE A LITTLE TRICKY AS WE WANT THEM TO CURVE TO MAKE OUR CIRCLE LOOK LIKE A SPHERE.

4

ADD AS MUCH DETAIL AS YOU LIKE TO THE SIDES!

HOW TO DRAW ALIEN EXPRESSIONS

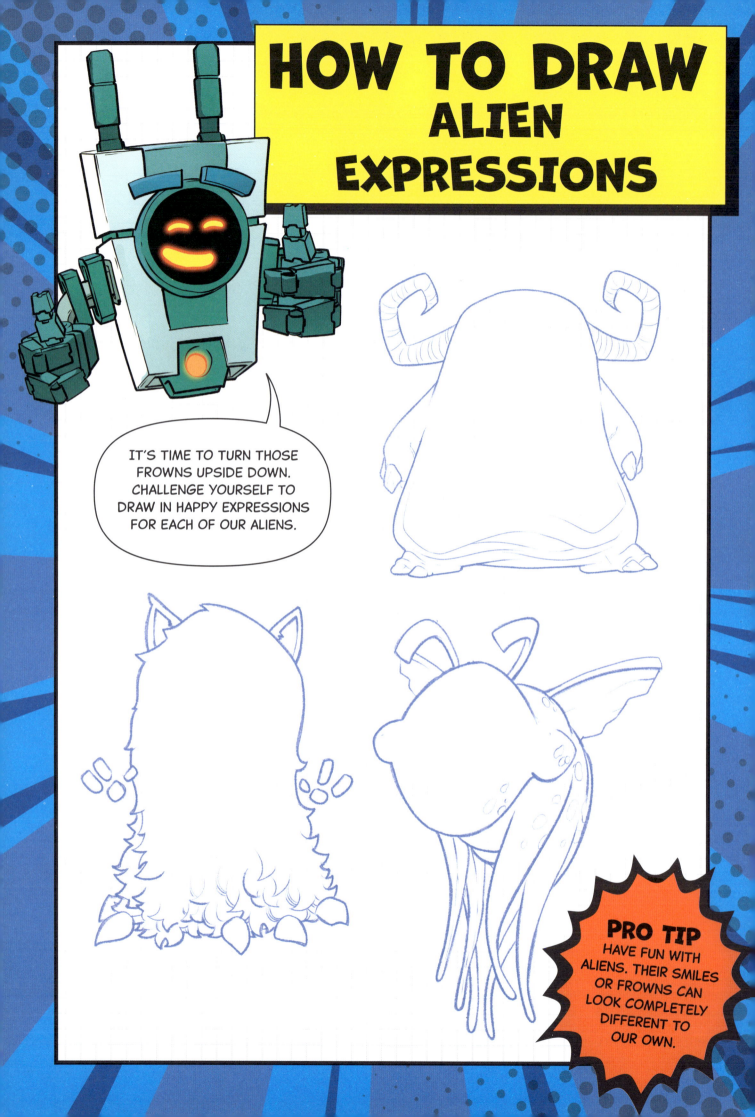

IT'S TIME TO TURN THOSE FROWNS UPSIDE DOWN. CHALLENGE YOURSELF TO DRAW IN HAPPY EXPRESSIONS FOR EACH OF OUR ALIENS.

PRO TIP
HAVE FUN WITH ALIENS. THEIR SMILES OR FROWNS CAN LOOK COMPLETELY DIFFERENT TO OUR OWN.

HOW TO DRAW
A SPACESHIP

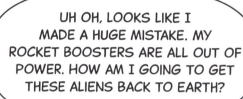

UH OH, LOOKS LIKE I MADE A HUGE MISTAKE. MY ROCKET BOOSTERS ARE ALL OUT OF POWER. HOW AM I GOING TO GET THESE ALIENS BACK TO EARTH?

LET'S DRAW WILL AND THE TEAM A SPACESHIP.

1

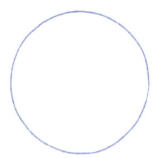

FIRST, LET'S DRAW A PORTHOLE WINDOW WITH A SIMPLE CIRCLE.

2

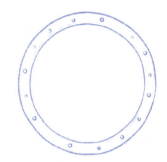

ADD IN A METAL RIM AND SOME SMALL SCREWS.

3

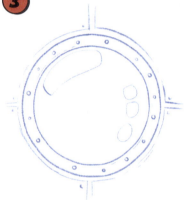

ADD SOME DETAIL, INCLUDING SOME HIGHLIGHTS ON THE GLASS.

1

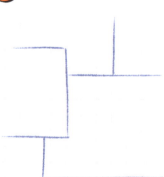

NEXT, LET'S DRAW SOME METAL PANELS. START WITH SOME SIMPLE SQUARES.

2

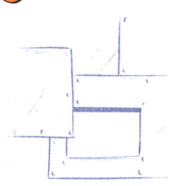

ADD SCREWS AROUND THE EDGE AND MAYBE ANOTHER PANEL FOR SOME TECH.

3

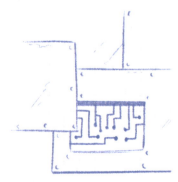

DRAW TECH CIRCUITRY WITH THESE LINE PATTERS.

YOU HAVE LEARNED HOW TO DRAW SO MUCH AS WE'VE CREATED OUR STORY. NOW IT'S TIME TO TEST YOURSELF AND DRAW IT ALL IN HERE ONE LAST TIME.

ALIENS, EXPRESSIONS, SUPERPOWERS . . .
YOU CAN DO IT ALL NOW!